Inside the World's Most Famous Intelligence Agencies

Inside Britain's MI6
Military Intelligence 6

Shaun McCormack

The Rosen Publishing Group, Inc.
New York

Published in 2003 by The Rosen Publishing Group, Inc.
29 East 21st Street, New York, NY 10010

Copyright © 2003 by The Rosen Publishing Group, Inc.

First Edition

All rights reserved. No part of this book may be reproduced in any form without permission in writing from the publisher, except by a reviewer.

Library of Congress Cataloging-in-Publication Data

McCormack, Shaun.
Britain's MI6: military intelligence 6 / by Shaun McCormack.— 1st ed.
   p. cm. — (Inside the world's most famous intelligence agencies)
Summary: Presents Britain's Military Intelligence 6 (MI6) as newly focused against terrorist networks throughout the world.
Includes bibliographical references and index.
ISBN   978-1-4358-9040-4
1. Great Britain. Secret Intelligence Service—History—Juvenile literature. [1. Great Britain. Secret Intelligence Service.]
I. Title. II. Series.
UB271.G7 M38 2003
327.1241—dc21

2002008053

Manufactured in the United States of America

Cover image: Britain's Secret Intelligence Service, also known as MI6, is based in this building at Vauxhall Cross in London, England. Its staff is responsible for gathering intelligence beyond Britain's borders. The primary role of MI6 is to uncover secret information that concerns Britain's security, defense, and foreign and economic policies.

INSIDE THE WORLD'S MOST FAMOUS INTELLIGENCE AGENCIES

Contents

	Introduction	4
Chapter One	The Beginning	6
Chapter Two	1900-1945	14
Chapter Three	1950-1991	22
Chapter Four	MI6 Structure in the Modern Day	34
Chapter Five	The Future	45
	Glossary	54
	For More Information	57
	For Further Reading	59
	Bibliography	60
	Index	62

Introduction

The British navy has long been considered one of the strongest military organizations in the world. Until 1909, Britain depended primarily on the Naval Intelligence Division (NID) to gather intelligence. Distributing detailed questionnaires to Royal Navy captains, the NID based its intelligence on their answers.

In 1909, Britain was rife with rumors that the Germans were planning an attack on British soil. When an NID mission to photograph a German military harbor that year failed, two naval captains were arrested. The scandal led the Royal Navy to take a hard look at its intelligence-gathering abilities, and ultimately to decide that they must create a separate, modernized organization that would be dedicated to gathering military intelligence.

The British Secret Intelligence Service (SIS), also known as Military Intelligence 6 (MI6), was founded in October 1909 as the foreign section of the Secret Service Bureau. The first SIS assignment was to gather secret information about German military plans. Years later, after World War II, MI6, in collaboration with the U.S. Central Intelligence Agency (CIA), concentrated its efforts on threats from Communist Russia, uncovering priceless, highly secret documents about the structure of the Soviet regime and its military strength.

Ian Fleming's book character James Bond became most people's idea of a British spy. Sean Connery starred as the first James Bond in the 1962 movie *Dr. No*. Eighteen more Bond movies followed. Actors who have portrayed James Bond on the silver screen include Roger Moore, Timothy Dalton, and, most recently, Pierce Brosnan.

The British Secret Intelligence Service, one of the most revered in the world, set the tone and backdrop for the rakish superspy James Bond, the book and movie character created by Ian Fleming in 1952. Fleming, once a British spy, was known for his imaginative and flamboyant James Bondesque lifestyle. Because British officials have refused to allow anything, including a freedom of information act, to undermine its secrecy, very little direct information is available about the British Secret Intelligence Service.

Chapter One
The Beginning

Intelligence gathering is the process by which nations learn about the military and political activities of other countries, using both overt (obvious) and covert (secretive) tactics. Since society began, nations have tried to protect themselves by learning what was happening inside and outside their borders. This was done overtly through diplomacy. But a desire for valuable information from secretive military and political organizations has led to the formation of covert intelligence-gathering services around the world.

Nations often build secret military intelligence networks with help from international business travelers and politicians. These people can become good intelligence agents because they are often able to gain access to important, valuable, or sensitive information from foreign countries while discussing business ventures and opportunities, or political issues. If intelligence agents are good at their jobs, no one will ever know that they are gathering military information. They will appear to be discussing simple business or political issues while the true purpose of their visits is to record conversations or take pictures with hidden microphones and cameras supplied by the military of top-secret documents.

The Beginning

It can take years for a bureau to establish a solid network of agents who are able to hide their real agendas and earn the trust of those they are observing. Agents must build up credibility with foreign businesspeople and politicians to gain access to sensitive information. But once agents gain the confidence of the people they spy on, they can uncover priceless information for their secret intelligence services. Top agents earn huge amounts of money doing this; secret military information is very valuable.

This tiny Minox camera, shown here in 1952, was designed in 1936 by Latvian Walter Zapp, who intended it to be handy for photography hobbyists. Instead, it became hugely popular with spies, especially those who wanted to photograph secret documents.

Establishing intelligence networks is hard enough, but administering these networks may be even more difficult. Once the flow of information starts, officers must decide how to use it. Professional intelligence officers are responsible for evaluating information for accuracy and deciding to whom it would be most useful. These officers must be able to think quickly. They have to know whom they can trust.

Military information can be extremely harmful if it is passed into the wrong hands. It is especially dangerous if information is given to a double agent—a person who works for two or more intelligence agencies. Double agents work for one agency and sell that agency's secrets to another for huge profits.

Britain's Queen Elizabeth II and Prime Minister Tony Blair stand on the steps of Blair's official residence at 10 Downing Street in London. This photo was taken on April 29, 2002, as the queen was beginning to celebrate her Golden Jubilee year, marking her fiftieth anniversary on the throne.

Formation of the U.K.

The need for military intelligence has long been important to the British. The United Kingdom has existed as a unified nation since the tenth century. It came into being after the union of England and Wales was enacted under the Statute of Rhuddlan in 1284. In 1707, England and Scotland agreed to join permanently as Great Britain in the Act of Union. Ireland entered the union in 1801. The current name of the country, the United Kingdom of Great Britain and Northern Ireland, was adopted in 1927.

Today, Britain is governed by a constitutional monarchy. The current chief of state is Queen Elizabeth II, who assumed that role on February 6, 1952; the heir apparent is Prince Charles, the queen's son. He was born on November 14, 1948. The Prime Minister is Anthony C. L. (Tony) Blair. Parliament is divided into two sections—the House of Commons and the House of Lords—and is staffed by representatives from these two houses. A general election is held every five years. British Parliament regulates government action in the UK. No statute may go into law or be repealed without the Parliament's consent. Tony Blair has been Prime Minister since the Labour Party took majority control of Parliament in 1997. As of this writing, the most recent election took place on June 7, 2001. Because Tony Blair's Labour Party received more votes than any other party, he retained his position as Prime Minister.

Origin of the SIS

Because the Naval Intelligence Division of the Royal Navy conducted early British intelligence gathering, British authorities believed that a naval captain would be best suited to head the first Secret Intelligence Service. Royal Navy Chief Mansfield Cumming (known to his colleagues as "C") was chosen as the organization's first head officer.

Born on April 1, 1859, Cumming became a cadet at the Royal Naval College in Osborne when he was thirteen years old. He joined his first ship, the HMS *Bellerophon*, in June of 1878.

Cumming suffered from seasickness throughout his life, a terrible ailment for a naval officer. Naval officials in 1885 decided that he was unfit for naval service, so he was assigned to an administrative role with the Royal Navy. Cumming served at naval bases along England's coast and accepted the job as head of the foreign section of the SIS on October 1, 1909. His office was the center for British intelligence gathering on Germany.

Some of Cumming's practices have become British intelligence traditions. For example, he initialed papers that crossed his desk in green ink. British intelligence officers still do this today. Because he was chief of the secret service, he was referred to as "C." This is the nickname given to all secret service chiefs who have followed him.

On October 3, 1914, shortly after the start of World War I in Europe, a tragic car accident in France established Cumming as a living legend. The wreck earned him the reputation of being the toughest chief the SIS has ever known.

Cumming was traveling on that day in a car driven by his son. The car smashed into a tree and overturned. Cumming's son Alexander was thrown through the windshield from the impact. The chief was trapped in the car. Legend says that he cut off his own leg with a penknife in an effort to escape the car and save his son. Alexander died in the accident, and the chief was left to hobble around on a wooden leg for the rest of his life. Hospital records show, however, that Cumming broke both of his legs in the accident. His left foot was amputated the day after the accident. For the rest of his life, Cumming intimidated SIS officers by tapping his wooden leg during meetings and conversations.

SIS and NID

It takes time and money to establish an effective worldwide intelligence organization. Before the SIS was even five years old, World War I had begun. Cumming did not have time to train agents or set up a network. As a result, the SIS got off to a slow start while the power of the NID grew. The Naval Intelligence Division already had a complex network of overseas spies in position. So most intelligence-gathering resources were passed on to the NID. By August 1, 1914, the day World War I officially began, the NID had agents in strategic positions around the globe. They monitored and recorded military shipping movements. The network of agents acted as a human radar chain.

Early Intelligence-Gathering Tactics

By the end of 1916, however, SIS and other Allied intelligence organizations, including those of France, Italy, Russia, and the United States, had established a network of train watchers that could monitor the movements of almost every German military troop. They recorded troop movements from behind enemy lines. People traveled mostly by train in those days. Aviation was in its early stages and trains were the fastest way to move soldiers from place to place. Agents passed military intelligence back into Allied territory with trained carrier pigeons.

Because wireless communication technology was in its infancy at the onset of World War I, British intelligence officers devised clever communication tactics. Military questionnaires were floated into German territory with balloons. Citizens who found the questionnaires were asked to answer them and float them back when the wind was blowing in the right direction.

Allied intelligence services operated escape lines for fleeing prisoners of war. By 1916, Allied intelligence

In this photo from World War I, Belgian soldiers attach a message to the leg of a carrier pigeon. During World War II, MI6 agents learned that Nazi-trained homing pigeons flying across Europe were transporting information vital to Hitler's British invasion plans. In response, MI6 trained an ace force of peregrine falcons to down the incoming pigeons.

controlled several escape lines and had smuggled large numbers of military officers back into British territory. It was well known that the officers brought sensitive intelligence information with them. Eventually Germany destroyed these escape paths.

Germany succeeded in destroying some of the Allied intelligence networks in 1915 and 1916. The crackdown on escape paths helped German authorities convict 235 Allied agents of espionage by the end of World War I. About 55 of the 235 agents were linked to the SIS.

World War I ended on November 11, 1918. The SIS had performed very well. Although just five years old when the war began, the organization had already established intelligence stations in Holland, France, and Egypt. Cumming proved that the new agency could work well with other global intelligence agencies. SIS had effectively combated counterespionage, interrogated prisoners, gathered information from behind enemy lines, and organized escape routes for fleeing prisoners of war. SIS also opened a New York office and established a network of agents in Russia.

Chapter Two
1900-1945

Britain's military powers had begun to weaken in the mid- to late-1800s. During Queen Victoria's reign (1837–1901), the country assumed that its strong navy would maintain military supremacy and the nation's superpower status. During the Boer War (1899–1902), British settlers defeated Dutch settlers in the battle to control South Africa. Even though the British outnumbered the Dutch, there were horrific casualties. Fierce criticism at home led Britain to analyze its intelligence efforts. By 1907, the Committee of Imperial Defence (CID), led by Rear-Admiral Sir Charles Ottley and his assistant Maurice Hankey, reviewed Britain's intelligence organization and discovered that there was not a single British agent on the entire mainland of Europe. The investigation was kept so secret that most countries still believed that Britain possessed the most extensive and sophisticated spy service in the world.

In May 1910, Reginald "Blinker" Hall, a rear admiral of the British navy, was granted permission by Admiral Sir Edmond Slade to begin a covert mission to photograph German naval efforts on the Frisian Island of Borkum, near the River Ems. Hall was first a Royal Navy officer. He established Room 40 at the Admiralty Building in London, where he led a network of cryptographers and code breakers who intercepted German communications that revealed the

This photo from 1900 shows wounded British soldiers in a squalid wagon house at Klip Drift in South Africa during the Boer War.

locations of Germany's warships throughout WW I. While two British spies involved in the covert mission were arrested by German police, put on trial, and sentenced to four years in jail for espionage, Hall was not arrested.

World War I and After

1914-1918

Up until 1914, the port of Gotenborg in Sweden usually required the presence of one British consul-general. By the end of 1914, thirty-three had been stationed there. World War I raged in Europe, as Britain, France, Russia , Italy , and the United States (the Allies) fought Germany, Austria-Hungary,

Bulgaria, and the Ottoman Empire (the Central Powers). Lord Horatio Herbert Kitchener reorganized the British War Office in 1915, returning the Secret Intelligence Service to its control. The British Imperial Security Intelligence Service (MO5) was renamed MI5. Four separate units were organized: MI1x for organization and administration, MI1a for operational intelligence, MI1b for censorship and propaganda, and MI1c for secret service and security. Counterespionage, which is the process by which one country fights other countries' intelligence-gathering efforts, became routine by 1916.

1919–1923

MI5 and SIS (MI6) operated independently of each other, although officials in London's intelligence bureaucracy considered the idea of combining them. The Secret Service Committee was formed to determine a peacetime operating procedure for the organizations. MI5 was given the responsibility of counterespionage, counter-sabotage, and counter-subversion in the U.K. and abroad. The Secret Intelligence Service was set up to deal with all other areas of intelligence. Its peacetime budget was set at £125,000 British (the equivalent of about $2 million today) a year, nearly half the wartime budget. SIS was given more responsibility for international intelligence and security threats.

1924–1938

The death of SIS Chief Mansfield Cumming in 1923 brought the appointment of Hugh Sinclair, who had joined the Royal Navy in 1886 and rose quickly through its ranks. Sinclair slowed SIS espionage efforts in Soviet Russia. He had

The British had expected an easy victory over the Turks in World War I. But when British Secretary of War Lord Kitchener visited Gallipoli, Turkey (he's pictured here in the trenches in 1915), and saw the terrible suffering among the British soldiers, he recommended that the British army withdraw. The British removed their troops so quietly that the Turks were completely surprised. Despite their defeat by the Turkish army, the British considered their secret evacuation a great military victory!

inherited an organization in financial turmoil. The reduced peacetime budget forced him to cut back and close down intelligence stations.

It is generally accepted that Sinclair focused too heavily on the rise of communism in Russia. This created a lapse in espionage activity in and against Germany, which gave the Nazi regime more freedom to grow without being watched.

The rise to power of the Nazis in Germany during the 1930s led to a heavy demand for emigration visas to Palestine.

It was well known that the Nazi Party and its leader, Adolf Hitler, were bent on destroying Europe's Jewish population. Jews believe that Palestine, now the nation of Israel, is their ancestral homeland. It is located on the eastern coast of the Mediterranean Sea in southwestern Asia. About 144,000 Jews, most of them from Germany, immigrated to Palestine in the 1930s in order to escape religious persecution. Many Jews in the path of the German war machine tried fleeing to friendly territories out of fear that they would be enslaved and tortured in Nazi concentration camps. Britain placed heavy restrictions on immigration in order to appease Arabs, but many Jews still made it to Palestine.

At the time, Palestine was a territory administered by Britain for the League of Nations. Britain required all prospective immigrants to provide proof of assets totaling $10,000 so that they would not be a financial burden on taxpayers when they arrived in Palestine. Three clerks recruited in Nicosia by Britain were found to be running a private service for Jews who were unable to meet the financial qualifications.

In the United Kingdom, passport control offices were overwhelmed by requests for visas to Palestine. A large number of people unable to meet the financial qualifications resorted to offering bribes to Passport Control Office (PCO) staff. This came to light September 4, 1936, when British intelligence officials discovered Major Hugh Reginald Dalton at The Hague in the Netherlands had committed suicide. When news of Dalton's death reached Sinclair, he ordered an immediate investigation, which uncovered several discrepancies in Dalton's accounts. SIS bookkeeper Percy Sykes and other unit officials decided

This photo shows German dictator Adolf Hitler during his victory parade through Vienna, Austria, on June 16, 1938. Five months later, on November 9 and 10, the German state sponsored pogroms in Germany and Austria in which the Nazis looted and destroyed synagogues and Jewish-owned businesses. This horrific event is known as Kristallnacht.

Dalton had taken his own life because he was guilty of taking bribes from Jews who wanted to enter Palestine.

1938: Anschluss

Anschluss is the term given to the annexation of Austria by Germany. In March of 1938, the German Army marched into Austria and took over the country. Five months later, on August 17, Captain Thomas Kendrick, SIS station head in Vienna, was arrested in Austria by the Gestapo, the Nazi police. Kendrick was an MI6 agent working undercover in Austria as the chief passport officer. MI6 was using Kendrick and the passport office

Here are German soldiers during World War II sending secret messages with the Enigma cryptographic machine. The Germans thought the Enigma code was unbreakable. But several brilliant Polish mathematicians, working with hundreds of analysts in Britain, decoded enough Enigma messages to help give the Allies a crucial advantage over the Germans.

to help prisoners of war escape to Allied territory. Britain was able to gather valuable information through this setup as agents interviewed war prisoners who had been trapped behind enemy lines. The prisoners who escaped from Nazi occupation provided Britain with information about the German military that they had observed while they were captive in German territory.

Sinclair was upset by Kendrick's arrest. He feared that if the Germans had discovered Kendrick, a top MI6 official, they would also uncover MI6's espionage and war prisoner escape path efforts. Kendrick, who had spent more than a dozen years with SIS, denied that he made any statements to the Gestapo, the German internal security police, during the Nazi regime. But reports in German newspapers made it clear that the chief passport officer's dual role was well known in Vienna. As a result, MI6 staff was withdrawn from British intelligence stations in Berlin, Germany, and Prague, Czechoslovakia (now the Czech Republic). Sinclair did this because he feared other top officials would be uncovered.

1939–1945: World War II

World War II began on September 1, 1939, when Germany invaded Poland. In return, Britain and France declared war on Germany on September 3. The fall of France in 1940 had disastrous effects on British intelligence. Czechoslovakia, Austria, and Poland had already fallen to the Germans. Norway, Denmark, Holland, Belgium, and the Balkans were on their way down. SIS was left with few neutral positions in Europe from which to run its intelligence efforts. British Prime Minister Winston Churchill formed his war cabinet on May 10, 1940, which had strong feelings about the supervision and operations of Britain's secret intelligence organizations.

At the onset of World War II, the British Secret Intelligence Service, also known as MI6, began an around-the-clock effort to decipher intercepted military transmissions by the enemy in Europe and Asia. Most of the enemy codes were produced on the German Enigma cryptographic machine. The British effort to crack the code was centered at the Government Code and Cypher School at Bletchley Park, near London. As the Military Intelligence's Signals Intelligence (MISI) effort grew, it was informally given the designation of MI8. Eventually, MI8, successful in cracking the Enigma code, provided the so-called ultra intelligence to Allied commanders and leaders which helped to shorten the war. Churchill later called MI8's code-cracking efforts "the secret weapon that won the war."

Chapter Three
1950-1991

After World War II, Berlin was divided into four sectors. The Russians, Americans, British, and French each controlled a portion of the city. The Russians controlled the largest part, which covered most of eastern Berlin. The citizens of Berlin traveled freely between all the sectors until 1952, when the borders were closed between East and West Germany. In 1961, after a disastrous summit meeting between American president Kennedy and Soviet premier Khrushchev, the East German government built the wall that completely surrounded West Berlin. During the wall's existence, about 5,000 people successfully "escaped" into West Berlin, 192 people were killed trying to cross, and around 200 were seriously injured.

Communist Russia began to extend its influence over Eastern Europe and North Korea during the 1950s. This led the United States and Communist Russia to become involved in what is known as the Cold War. A constant state of nonviolent hostility, the Cold War apparently ended with the collapse of Soviet Russia in 1991.

After World War II, MI6 returned its focus to espionage in the Soviet Union. The British MI6 and the American Central Intelligence Agency (CIA) were linked together in a number of operations between 1950 and the present. Both nations were bent on stopping the spread of communism in Europe, believing that it threatened the existence of democracy.

In this photo from 1963, American president John F. Kennedy visits the Berlin Wall, where he made his now famous speech in which he declared, "Ich bin ein Berliner." After calling himself a "Berliner," he promised to defend the residents of the city's western portion, which had been surrounded completely by the Communist-built wall.

By the end of 1950, MI6 was convinced that the Soviet Union was intent on war. In 1952, the British League for European Freedom (BLEF) helped organize a major conference for Eastern European exile groups. The conference was sponsored by the Central and East European Commission of the European Movement (EM), an organization that dealt only with countries outside of the Soviet border.

The conference was paid for by undisclosed private funds. The involvement of Warren Fugitt of the American Committee for a United Europe, along with Roger Bull, W. Griffith, and John Leich from the U.S. National Committee for a Free Europe (NCFE), suggests that the CIA was the true source of funding.

The conference led to the creation of a European Fund for Exiles. The fund's administration was a front group. It posed as an organization to assist student exiles in continuing their studies. It was really an intelligence effort to stop the spread of communism. The bringing together of exiles provided a powerful propaganda machine. News about it was spread throughout the Soviet bloc by NCFE-supported radio stations, the BBC (British Broadcasting Corporation), and exile press outlets.

By 1953, MI6 began to pull itself away from the support of exiles and stopped funding many groups. A year later, Britain's leadership withdrew its efforts from issues concerning Soviet matters, leaving the British League for European Freedom leadership to the United States. BLEF's influence faded throughout the 1950s and 1960s, and was represented in the 1970s by the right-wing World Anti-Communist League.

During his study of the intelligence efforts during the Cold War, Trevor Barnes wrote that MI6 was running its own operations to encourage unity in Europe. The principal interest of

On the left, from 1948, is Duncan Sandys, Joint Secretary of the European Movement. On the right is Major-General Sir Stewart Menzies, with his bride in 1932. Menzies headed the British Secret Service from 1939 until he retired in 1951.

MI6 was to use the European Movement as an anticommunist front group. It was part of MI6's effort to shape the postwar world into a conservative, anticommunist entity.

Evidence suggests that one objective of MI6's EM involvement may have been to fight federalists who advocate a form of government in which a union of states recognizes a central authority while maintaining certain individual governing powers. Records show that key EM officials such as Joseph Retinger and Duncan Sandys were in contact with MI6 chief Stewart Menzies and received covert assistance from MI6. Through close relationships with Sandys, Retinger, and other influential agents, MI6 was able to penetrate major federalist groups like EM and identify allies. It served as a useful way to monitor influential politicians in Europe during the Cold War.

The American CIA, which was also trying to prevent the spread of communism, was much wealthier than MI6. British intelligence officers cooperated with the CIA in projects to investigate European anticommunist spy networks.

Intelligence agents were also involved in anticommunist groups aimed at teens. The European Youth Coalition (EYC) was born in the 1950s and flourished in the 1960s. Its purpose was to undermine Soviet efforts to influence political opinions of the young. MI6 worked inside the EYC to unify noncommunist groups in Western Europe. In 1967 it was revealed that the United States was linked to the EYC. An investigation found that the American Foundation for Youth and Students Abroad had funded the EYC. Almost all of the EYC's money came from the United States. CIA officials denied any involvement until 1975, when Thomas Braden, the former head of the CIA's International Organizations Division, admitted that the CIA had funded both the EM and the EYC.

A secret MI6 document dated July 17, 1956, showed the extent of MI6 and CIA influence on the anticommunist International Student Coalition (ISC). On the surface, the ISC was an organization dedicated to discussing education

In 1975, former CIA executive Thomas Braden revealed that the CIA had channeled thousands of dollars through the leaders of American labor unions to help European labor unions resist the lure of communism in postwar Europe.

and problems encountered by students. However, it is generally accepted that these humanistic efforts were just a front. ISC was actually a product of Cold War espionage. It was bent on fighting communism. ISC published anticommunist magazines and pamphlets and organized student rallies to sway teens away from communism. Eastern European nations were not admitted to the organization because it was an anticommunism group and Eastern European nations were under communist influence.

A document from June 1960 revealed that MI6 had recruited ISC students in commonwealth countries, a loose federation made up of countries that had once been Soviet republics. MI6 received help from commonwealth intelligence agencies in running the operation. For fifteen years, the CIA was the biggest contributor to the ISC. The CIA, an American intelligence agency, funneled funds to ISC to support anticommunist operations. The official source of funding was the U.S. National Student Association (NSA), but this organization was really a CIA front group set up to fund anticommunist efforts in Eastern Europe.

While Eastern European nations were excluded from the ISC, anticommunist intelligence agencies still sought intelligence from within these nations. The CIA was able to maintain control over the ISC because all projects had to be submitted to the NSA for budget approval. Between 1962 and 1964, the CIA-financed New York Fund for Youth and Student Affairs contributed nearly $1.8 million to the ISC.

The 1960s were the best and worst of times for MI6's involvement with the American CIA. Several intelligence-gathering accomplishments drew the admiration of the United States. This was good for MI6 because the CIA could

Scotland Yard issued this photograph of double-agent George Blake in 1966 after he escaped from Wormwood Scrubs prison by climbing over the wall. Blake had been sentenced to forty-two years in the maximum security jail. Upon reaching Moscow, he was awarded the Order of Lenin.

provide them with the financing and technology that MI6 could not afford on its own. But this was overshadowed by continual mole hunts to determine the names and duties of counterintelligence agents within MI6 and revealed its inner workings to the United States.

Beginning in 1958, MI6 had three undercover agents working inside Urzad Bezpieczenstwa (UB), the Polish secret intelligence service. The most noted agent was code-named Noddy. Poland's close relationship with the Russian KGB meant that MI6 could watch the inner workings of the Russian intelligence agency through the intelligence gathering of Noddy and the other two agents. MI6 passed KGB information to CIA officials, who called this information some of the most valuable intelligence ever collected.

The CIA rewarded the work of MI6 by paying $20 million for them to further their covert intelligence efforts in Poland. The overflow of cash led to over-eagerness on the part of MI6, and ultimately to the exposure of MI6's assistance to the CIA.

Double agents Oleg Penkovsky and George Blake created tremendous problems for MI6 and the CIA at this time. Penkovsky was a high-ranking Soviet official who worked for both MI6 and the CIA. Blake worked for MI6 and funneled information to the KGB. Blake blew the cover on hundreds of western agents when he provided detailed information to Soviet Intelligence (KGB) about the MI6 and CIA. The CIA feared that Blake's confession to the KGB might blow the cover on Penkovsky's operations. Penkovsky was a double agent for Britain. As a Soviet agent, he had access to Soviet intelligence which he funneled to MI6. When he was finally caught, it was great loss.

In this 1963 photo, Oleg Penkovsky has just been sentenced to death by firing squad in Moscow. He had admitted to spying for Britain with British businessman Greville Wynne, who was sentenced to eight years in prison.

Penkovsky supplied CIA and MI6 officials with 111 roles of film and 10,000 pages of KGB intelligence reports. The reports contained information about Soviet nuclear and missile technologies—subjects that the West had known little about. Penkovsky also identified 400 to 500 Soviet Military Intelligence (GRU) officers and another 200 to 300 KGB officers. His reports included profiles on the personalities of almost every agent he identified. From these reports and profiles and a later addition of a Kremlin telephone directory, an MI6 specialist on the Soviet Union was able to produce the first ever chain-of-command profile of the Soviet hierarchy. Penkovsky had helped lift the veil of secrecy surrounding Kremlin operations.

Seeing a similar photo in October 1962, American president John Kennedy demanded that Russian premier Nikita S. Khrushchev remove all missiles from Cuba, an island ninety miles from Florida. Kennedy also ordered a naval blockade to prevent the Russians from bringing more missiles to Cuba. When Premier Khrushchev authorized his Soviet commanders to launch their nuclear weapons if the Americans invaded Cuba, the countries were deadlocked. After seven days, the Russian premier finally agreed to remove the missiles from Cuba. The Cuban Missile Crisis is considered the most critical and dangerous event of its time.

Penkovsky had destroyed the myth about Russia's intercontinental ballistic missiles. Before Penkovsky's espionage work, military officials believed Soviet missiles were capable of precision attacks from long range. They were not.

The Cuban Missile Crisis was a frightening conflict between the United States and USSR. It is believed to have been the closest the world had ever came to a nuclear war. When the United States discovered Cuba possessed Soviet nuclear missiles capable of hitting targets in the United States, as a result of a U-2 spy plane mission, it imposed a naval blockade on Cuba and demanded the Soviets remove the missiles. On October 19, 1962 (soon after the start of the

Cuban Missile Crisis), the CIA prepared a detailed report on the Soviet SS-4 missile.

The KGB entered Penkovsky's apartment the next day and recovered the spy camera he had used to photograph KGB documents. He was arrested on October 22 by the KGB. The CIA and MI6 officers concluded that this was a result of his being overused. But Penkovsky's intelligence reports helped the United States throughout the Cuban missile crises. As a result, the United States learned that the Soviet missiles were not capable of long-range attacks. Soon after, Penkovsky was executed by the KGB.

In the early 1960s, the intelligence community was also concerned about events in Vietnam. Communism had worked its way into North Vietnam and threatened South Vietnam. The United States, who wanted to stop the spread of communism, sent representatives to act as military advisers to South Vietnam. After the North Vietnamese attacked an American ship near its shores, the United States began bombing the region in March of 1965. MI6 helped the United States by forwarding intelligence reports from its station heads in Hanoi, Vietnam. MI6 secretly transferred a supply of weapons and war materials used to defeat the Malayan Communist Party to South Vietnamese troops. This, however, provided little help because the United States was never very successful with its anticommunist propaganda efforts in South Vietnam. Many South Vietnamese did not want to fight the North Vietnamese. America's propaganda campaigns could not generate enough interest to have any real effect against North Vietnam.

Budget cutbacks and Cold War concentration in the 1970s put MI6 into a touchy position. In the late 1970s,

In the 1978 picture (on the left) is Percy Cradock. As foreign policy adviser to British prime minister Margaret Thatcher (shown on the right in 1980), Cradock contended that the Cold War would go on forever. But the Berlin Wall came down in 1989, and the USSR fell apart a few years later, highlighting the poor quality of the intelligence gathered by MI6 in the late 1980s.

MI6's Latin American stations were consolidated into one station based in Buenos Aires, Argentina. Mark Heathcote was head of the Buenos Aires station in 1980.

Heathcote had several reliable sources in Buenos Aires, but none of them were able to gain access to the inner circle of the Junta, the group of military officers who had seized control of the government of Argentina. The lack of sensitive-intelligence gathering led MI6 officers to underestimate Argentina's new ambitions. Changes in Argentina's goals in the late 1970s and early 1980s were more evident in the media than in intelligence reports.

British prime minister Margaret Thatcher more than doubled government spending on intelligence in the 1980s. Thatcher supported MI6 more than any prime minister had since the end of World War II. Newspapers and other media outlets reported that MI6 was spreading its intelligence nets throughout the world, but the Soviet Union was still its primary focus. In 1985, Thatcher's foreign policy advisor, Percy Cradock, said the Cold War would "go on forever" and insisted that the Soviets were still bent on "world domination." When Mikhail Gorbachev was elected to head the Soviet Union, Cradock believed it was a subversive political plot to trick the world into thinking the Soviets were beginning to back down from the threat of starting World War III.

The mindset that Cradock created within the intelligence community prevented MI6 from understanding the true political tides in Eastern Europe and the Soviet Union. So when East German border guards began breaking down the Berlin Wall on November 10, 1989, MI6 was shocked. The fall of the Berlin Wall was a symbolic end to the Soviet empire. It became obvious that fear and a lack of quality intelligence gathering led MI6 to overestimate the Soviet economy and military budget. Ultimately, the Soviet Union collapsed in 1991, ending the Cold War.

In February 1998, senior U.S. intelligence officers confirmed to the *Los Angeles Times* that the CIA and MI6 plotted in 1995 to have Iraqi president Saddam Hussein assassinated. By providing intelligence, finance, and arms, they assisted opposition groups in northern and southern Iraq with attempted coups and bombing campaigns.

Chapter Four
MI6 Structure in the Modern Day

MI6, which stands for Military Intelligence, Section 6, is the modern-day version of the SIS. According to most sources, Richard Billing Dearlove now heads the MI6. Dearlove became involved with espionage after graduating from college. He worked as MI6's assistant chief before assuming the role of "C."

The BBC reported in February 1999 that Dearlove was selected by British foreign secretary Robin Cook and Prime Minister Tony Blair from a short list of candidates drawn from inside and outside the MI6. Although Dearlove's election as the new "C" was made public (it was only the second time MI6 had ever made a "C" appointment public), a photograph was not released. The world does not know what Dearlove looks like.

Dearlove was born in Cornwall, England, on January 23, 1945. He attended the private Monkton Combe School, spent a year at Kent School in Connecticut in the United States (1962–1963), and then went to Queen's College in Cambridge, England.

Dearlove joined MI6 when he was twenty-one years old. He received his first foreign posting in 1968 to Nairobi, Kenya. Dearlove was chosen to head up the MI6's Washington, D.C., station in 1991.

British newspapers reported that Dearlove's appointment reflected a new commitment in the post–Cold War era to combat international organized crime. Dearlove earns somewhere between £98,400 and £168,910 per year (or between $153,351 and $263,246).

The British Foreign Office released little information about Dearlove, but the BBC tracked down his residence in Putney, London, and spoke with his neighbors. A woman who asked the BBC to withhold her name said Mr. Dearlove and his family were so secretive that it had become amusing.

"It's been a joke with me and my husband, that the man next door was a spy. We've lived here two years and only met them once, we hardly ever see them," the woman told BBC reporters. She went on to say that she and her neighbors had received notes in their mailboxes asking them not to speak to reporters if asked about the Dearloves.

In addition to Dearlove, MI6 employs an estimated 2,300 workers and operates on an annual budget of £220 million ($338 million).

MI6's Responsibilities

MI6 is a foreign intelligence service. It deals only with matters outside of the United Kingdom. Domestic counterintelligence is handled by the MI5, short for Military Intelligence, Section 5.

The British Intelligence Services Act of 1994 says the job of an MI6 agent is "(a) to obtain and provide information relating to the actions or intentions of persons outside the British Islands; and (b) to perform other tasks relating to the actions or intentions of such persons . . . [in relation to] the interests of national security, with particular reference to defence and foreign policies . . . the interests of the economic well-being of the UK . . . or in support of the prevention or detection of serious crime."

The Intelligence Services Act of 1994 gave birth to the Parliamentary Intelligence and Security Committee (PISC). The PISC is responsible for overseeing the spending, administration, and policies of MI5 and MI6.

Current Intelligence Gathering

The advancement of communism in Russia, long a major concern for MI6, has faded away since the end of the Cold War. It had begun after World War II when the British and American alliance with the Soviet Union began to disintegrate. While the Soviets sought to expand communism in Europe and beyond, the British and Americans feared this was a threat to democracy. In turn, the Soviets were concerned about the spread of democracy throughout the world. Each side built up its military arsenals, including nuclear weaponry, as the possibly of war between them loomed on the horizon. Tensions often ran high. This period, which lasted until the collapse of the Soviet Union in 1991, is referred to as the Cold War. Britain's MI6 worked closely with America's CIA during the Cold War to stop the spread of communism in Eastern Europe and to learn about Russia's nuclear missile technology.

The last known confrontation between MI6 and Russia came in 1996 when one British spy and four British diplomats were thrown out of Russia. MI6 spy Rosemary Sharpe was accused of paying three German intelligence agents for information about Russian military equipment. The German agents failed to pass the money on to their superiors and were investigated for corruption. The investigation blew the covers on Sharpe and another British spy.

MI6 pays its employees based on performance. The more information they gather, the more money they make. This is done to motivate agents to uncover valuable intelligence. Agents who fail to achieve MI6 goals can be fired.

Like other intelligence agencies, MI6 acquires some information by setting up fake companies or political groups, called front groups. Front groups give MI6 the ability to put agents in places where they can gather valuable information. In this case, front means fake. A front works like a façade. People in front groups wear friendly masks to hide their true agendas.

In 1989, Soviet president Mikhail Gorbachev visited with British prime minister Margaret Thatcher in London, foreshadowing the end of the Cold War.

Front groups function in the same way that an individual agent does. Members must spend time establishing their covers. As an example, MI6 might gain access to information about Iraq's germ warfare capabilities by setting up agents in a phony chemical company. They will often hire people who have spent their lives working in the chemical industry. If the agents are successful, employees will have no idea that they are working for a front group. If employees are dedicated to what they believe is a job for a real chemical company, clients will believe they are buying goods from a company whose first interest is selling chemicals. By setting up a fake company and selling goods to those known to work with or for the Iraqi government, MI6 can learn where the chemicals are being sent. They can use that information to determine the location of military bases and the types of weapons that are being created. Combining this kind of operation with traditional detective-type work, MI6 is able to find out who owns the companies that produce the chemical weapons.

The MI6 is often involved in uncovering information on terrorist activities and plots. In recent years, Northern Ireland and the Irish Republican Army (IRA) have been key targets of MI6 intelligence-gathering operations. Six attacks in London were linked to the IRA from July 2000 to November 2001. A Russian-built Mark 22 anti-tank weapon attacked MI6 spy headquarters in central London in September 2000. A missile from the rocket launcher shattered an eighth-floor window of the MI6 building. British authorities suspected that the IRA was responsible for the bombing. Like most of the world's intelligence agencies, MI6 now focuses its efforts on terrorist networks throughout the world as a result of the terrorist attacks on the World Trade Center in New York City and on the Pentagon outside Washington, D.C., on September 11, 2001. British intelligence reported in February 2001 that top members of Osama bin Laden's Al Qaeda terrorist network, the organization accused of the terrorist attacks in the United States, were hiding in Lebanon. MI6 believes the Hezbollah terrorist network was assisting twenty or more senior Al Qaeda

On September 21, 2000, a small missile hit the upper floors of MI6 headquarters in London. In this photo, Alan Fry, head of the antiterrorist branch, speaks at a press conference in front of the MI6 building. He announced that the attack caused little damage to the building.

members. The Hezbollah was held responsible for the 1983 attack that killed 241 U.S. Marines in Beirut.

Musa Kusa, the head of Libyan leader Moammar Gadafi's External Security Organization, met with MI6 officials in February 2001. He identified more than a dozen Libyans living in the U.K. who have links to bin Laden's Al Qaeda network.

MI 5: Intelligence at Home

In the United Kingdom, MI5 and British police are seeking powers to seize all records of telephone calls, e-mails,

On October 23, 1983, a truck bomb struck the U.S. Marine barracks in Beirut, killing 241. The U.S. government has long considered Imad Fayez Mughniyah responsible for planning this and a long list of other atrocities. Mughniyah has eluded capture for twenty years.

and Internet connections made by every person living in British territory. They are demanding new legislation to keep a record of every phone call made in the country for as long as seven years back. The new intelligence efforts are being made to combat the growing problems associated with Internet crime. Computers have been used to run child pornography rings, by terrorists to recruit new members, and by international drug traffickers for banking. In a document uncovered by the British *Observer* newspaper, a government official admits that the legislation would clash with the Human Rights Act, which grants citizens certain rights to privacy. Critics argue that the new intelligence efforts defy laws that protect the public against intrusion into private lives.

Civil liberties and human rights advocates in the U.K. have warned British government officials against granting secret intelligence services the right to read private data transmissions. They say it gives the agencies too much power and violates human rights. Liberty, a U.K. human rights group, warned that the new legislation would breach the Human Rights Act and the Data Protection Act. Liberty also noted that if Britain's MI5 and MI6 abuse human rights, they could be forced into the European Court of Human Rights.

Liberty director John Waldman said: "The security services and the police have an immense appetite for collecting up information about our private lives, but this is an extraordinary idea. This would violate the principles of the Data Protection Act and the Human Rights act and the government should reject this idea now. If it goes ahead we will challenge this in the courts in this country and the European Court of Human Rights."

National Criminal Intelligence Service deputy director general Roger Gaspar wrote a document that describes the new spy plans. Gaspar said the digital spying system was necessary. He wrote: "We believe that the Home Office already accepts that such activity is unquestionably lawful, necessary and proportional, as well as being vital in the interest of justice."

The electronic database required to monitor and store all digital transmissions is said to cost about £3 million (about $3.7 million) to set up and £9 million (about $14 million) per year to run.

MI5's Responsibilities

MI5 acts much like the Federal Bureau of Investigation (FBI) in the United States. The major difference is that it does not have the authority to make arrests. MI5 must notify British legal authorities at Scotland Yard. British police are responsible for making arrests resulting from MI5's discoveries.

Its main objective has been to protect against the destruction and undermining of British organizations by foreign intelligence services within Britain. Lately, it has gained a wider power to monitor national security issues. Like MI6, its sister unit, MI5 is very concerned with Northern Ireland's desire for self-government. Former MI5 Director-General Stella Rimington expanded MI5's responsibilities to include the fight against organized crime. She stepped down in 1996 and was succeeded by Stephen Lander. As of October 2002, the new head will be Eliza Manningham-Buller. This was announced in May 2002.

The headquarters for MI5 are located in Thames House on Millbank in London. An estimated 1,850 men and women work for the security service. This is a drop from 2,150 employees that were employed by the organization in the late 1990s. The agency last reported its budget in 1999 as less than £140 million (about $215 million dollars) per year.

MI5 is divided into separate branches. Branch "A" deals with bugging, break-ins, and surveillance. Branch "B" handles personnel. Branch "C" concerns itself with the selection of government employees and state security offices. Another branch performs internal surveillance of subversives, trade unions, radical political groups, and terrorist groups like the IRA as well as counterespionage against suspected moles.

How MI5 Divides Its Budget Expenditures

- 39%   IRA and other Irish and domestic terrorism
- 33%   International terrorism within the U.K.
- 25%   Counterespionage
- 3%   Counter-subversion

MI5 Tactics

MI5 agents are masters of telephone-tapping. It has been reported that MI5 taps 30,000 telephone calls each year. It was reported in 1992 that there had been 102 security-service intrusion complaints filed over a three-year span. Security Service Commissioner Lord Justice Stuart-Smith said that ninety-nine of these complaints had no merit and that the other three cases were justified. Nearly forty civilian complaints were filed against MI5 in 1994. Authorities dismissed all of them.

Civil liberties have often appeared to be less important to the British government than national security. It appears that the British government overrides its citizens' right to privacy when they want to conduct investigations. MI5 is accused of keeping records on more than a million U.K. residents who they consider to be potentially dangerous. Laws forbid authorities from giving any information about surveillance to residents. In fact, authorities are forbidden

This photo from 1968 shows how a tap is placed in a telephone. In 1987, the British government tried to ban a book called *Spycatcher: The Candid Autobiography of a Senior Intelligence Officer*, in which the author detailed how British intelligence, with the blessing of the government, tapped phone conversations within the government's own agencies beginning in the 1960s. The goal was to uncover counterspies within MI5 and MI6.

from releasing any information about surveillance. If a person fears that the government is spying on them and seeks legal help, authorities are still not allowed to release any information to help them protect themselves. Liberal Democrat police security spokesman Alan Beith said any complaints about MI5 harassment will "just disappear into a black hole."

Chapter Five

The Future

Over the next several years, as the worldwide intelligence community plays a cat-and-mouse game with global terrorist organizations, it appears that technical intelligence gathering will move toward the Internet, and then away.

The Internet

Stories in newspapers and on television about secret intelligence information have been posted on the World Wide Web. In the U.K., the *Guardian* newspaper reported in May of 1999 that government officials were desperately trying to shut down a Web site where dozens of MI6 agents had been identified. The cover was blown on more than 100 agents. MI6 officials feared that the Web site had the potential to damage its worldwide operations.

The Web site, based in the United States, revealed the names of 117 people including several who were not MI6 agents. A second Web site identified nine MI6 agents named in a court document signed by Richard Tomlinson, a former MI6 officer. Tomlinson claimed that the agency was involved in a scandal that was responsible for the death of Princess Diana. Tomlinson received a barrage of e-mails and letters after his name was connected to the court document used in the list.

On February 17, 2001, British Foreign Secretary Robin Cook spoke at the Labour Party Spring Conference in Glasgow, Scotland. Britain had recently announced that the air raids it launched against Iraq in collaboration with the United States had been humanitarian actions.

The list of 117 names appeared on a Web site related to the *Executive Intelligence Review*, a publication that prints ideas about government conspiracy theories. The *Guardian* did not print the name of the Web site. It has been suggested that the newspaper withheld the Web site name because of threats from MI6.

The site was removed hours after the list was published. Many people believed Internet spying led to the quick discovery of the list, and that MI6 was responsible for the Web site being taken down.

The list included the names of current MI6 chief Richard Dearlove, former chief Sir David Spedding, and former MI6 Middle East controller Geoffrey Tantum. It included names of MI6 officers stationed in sensitive areas like the Balkans, where Tomlinson served as an MI6 agent. MI6 was especially concerned about the safety of agents in unstable areas because it would become harder to ensure their safety.

Foreign secretary Robin Cook said not all the names on the list were connected with MI6. "Nevertheless the release of any such list, however inaccurate it may be, is a deeply irresponsible and dangerous act," Cook said.

This security breach showed how dangerous the Internet can be as an intelligence weapon. But many people believe that within the next few years, little information on the Web will be considered top secret, because the Web itself is becoming more of a mainstream outlet for information.

This is why British officials are trying to pass legislation that will allow them to monitor Internet traffic. By doing this, they will be able to track known agents as they surf the Web. In most cases, MI6 will be able to block the posting of sensitive intelligence information before it is discovered. Tomlinson has told the British media that he believes the Internet will mean the end of the world's intelligence services. More than 100 copies of the agent list were published on the Web. The list was spread through the Web in chain e-mails. The chain was started in New Zealand by Peter Wills, a physics professor at the University of Auckland. Wills is a well known civil liberties, antinuclear, and Greenpeace campaigner.

When Wills was asked about balancing national security with civil liberties, he said: "None of these agents would be at risk if the British immediately withdrew them, disbanded MI6, and pensioned their agents off in respectable jobs (or handed those who had committed crimes in other countries over to the appropriate authorities for justice)."

"We used the technique of rapid email dispersal a few years ago when Nicky Hager published his book *Secret Power*. In the early hours before its publication I distributed copies to about 6 different locations internationally, rendering ineffective any injunction to halt distribution of the book the following morning," Wills said.

Over the next several years, the value of information distributed on the Web will change. Society as a whole will change. As more and more people become wired for the Web, sensitive intelligence quickly becomes common knowledge. As society becomes more dependent on the Internet, MI6 and other intelligence services will probably rely more on human intelligence than on advanced technology to conduct espionage. They especially don't want secret intelligence information printed in mass media outlets.

Fighting Terrorism

At the start of the new millennium, the task at hand is to locate terrorist networks and determine their activities. Once this is done, MI6 and others will attempt to infiltrate these organizations and halt their progress.

An enormous amount of intelligence staffing is needed to monitor terrorist movements. Up to this point, intelligence gathered about terrorist networks has been misinterpreted or ignored. Many small terrorist and militant groups have been underestimated. Large intelligence services, like large corporations, tend to be arrogant and shrug off security threats from what they believe are weak enemies.

A lack of cooperation between MI5, MI6, and the British police is to blame for many intelligence failures in the U.K. The organizations are in a power struggle and sometimes fail to communicate because of political grudges.

The terrorist attacks in the United States on September 11, 2001, were probably the biggest intelligence failure in the history of the United States. America was caught napping, and several thousand innocent people died. The attack showed the world how dangerous a small, organized group of militants could be when they succeed in intelligence gathering.

The World Trade Center towers collapsed after terrorists flew airliners into them on September 11, 2001. According to Peter Fray of the *London Herald*, MI6 agents had warned U.S. embassy staff in London about the plot two years earlier, after they received information that Osama bin Laden's followers were planning to use civilian aircraft in "unconventional ways, possibly as flying bombs."

Intelligence sources sent warnings to American government officials before the attacks in New York and Washington, D.C., but the warnings were not acted upon. They were considered vague, weak, or just talk.

Al Qaeda (Arabic for "the base") intelligence allegedly uncovered security lapses within America's airline companies. It was able to monitor flight paths and schedules. It uncovered architectural specifications of the World Trade Center's twin towers and used them to pinpoint structural weaknesses. By combining this intelligence, Al Qaeda militants were able to pull off the most horrific terrorist strike in the history of the world.

Besides killing thousands of people, wreaking havoc on the United States and the global economy, and terrorizing the entire world, the terrorist attacks of September 11 revealed a glaring need for better human-intelligence gathering and intelligence sharing.

Al Qaeda had been operating in Britain and the United States for years before the September 11 attacks. Established in 1988, the organization has executed military operations in South Africa, the Middle East, Europe, Asia, the Philippines, India, China, and now, the United States. The intelligence community believes Al Qaeda is developing links with other terrorist organizations throughout the world. It is believed that satellites and spy planes will not be enough to gather vital intelligence about Al Qaeda. While the intelligence community might be able to intercept phone calls with voice recognition technology or faxes and e-mails sent to and from Al Qaeda members, it might not be able to uncover sensitive information. This

British prime minister Tony Blair was the first Western leader to visit Afghanistan after the fall of the Taliban government. He is shown during this visit in January 2002 giving a press conference. Afghan interim president Hamid Karzai stands next to him. Behind them are soldiers from the International Security Assistance Force.

could occur because the terrorist networks have already made plans to avoid detection by technological means.

Most military information transmitted over the Web or wireless communication networks is sent using encryption, which blocks access to data. Encryption changes words into a slew of mixed symbols, numbers, and letters. Ideally, only the sender and recipient of the encrypted messages have the tools to decode the information. Most of the world's digital data spying tools are unable to read encrypted messages.

In the coming years, national intelligence organizations will focus on developing better human intelligence, although it will be very difficult to place operatives in key locations.

Mass media in the United States and Britain have printed stories about CIA and MI6 agents operating in Afghanistan. This is where military intelligence believes Al Qaeda officials were stationed when they launched the September 11 attack. The intelligence community is concerned that it is nearly impossible for a British or American undercover agent to blend into the tribal culture of the region.

One alternative is to work with Pakistan's Inner-Service Intelligence (ISI) organization, which has agents who understand Afghanistan's culture and speak its native Pushtu language. But there are fears that Al Qaeda has already infiltrated ISI. If ISI has been thoroughly infiltrated by Al Qaeda, MI6 will end up revealing more intelligence than it gathers by working with the Pakistani agency.

Despite the unknown value of technological intelligence and the significant lack of human intelligence in Afghanistan, MI6 staff will see an increase in its work with the U.S. National Security Agency (NSA) on the top-secret Echelon satellite spying system.

Echelon, a digital information watchdog, can read most e-mails and faxes and record telephone calls. Echelon analyzes data transmissions for thousands of keywords like "bomb" or "MI6" that might be used by terrorists and criminals. When a keyword is discovered, an Echelon agent reviews the phone call, e-mail, or fax. The biggest problem now is that the number of data transmissions red-flagged for review has skyrocketed because the entire world has been talking about the terrorist strikes in the United States. Intelligence officials will have to search through millions of transmissions.

The Future

At this point, it's unlikely that terrorists will discuss military plans through e-mail, on the Web, or in a telephone conversation. These are now insecure networks that can be easily monitored by technological espionage systems. Terrorists are aware that the world's intelligence agencies are spying on them, so they do their best to stay away from insecure communications devices.

It is safe to say that the world's intelligence agencies have become a lot busier as a result of the September 11 attacks. This will cost an enormous amount of money, with the burden falling on taxpayers. Individual privacy will take a backseat to national security, and everyone will have to contribute to the cause.

Glossary

administrative Business management duties.
Anschluss The annexation of Austria by Germany in 1938.
ballistic missile A flying weapon that is guided to hit a target in the distance.
BBC The British Broadcasting Corporation.
bloc A community.
chief of state The leader of the constitutional monarchy of the United Kingdom.
CIA The U.S. Central Intelligence Agency.
CID The Committee of Imperial Defense.
cold war A state of political tension and military rivalry that stops just short of full-blown warfare.
commonwealth A union of self-governing states.
counterespionage The process by which one country prevents another country's intelligence efforts.
covert Secretive, hidden, or undercover.
diplomacy The art of conducting international relations with tact and skill when dealing with people from other cultures.
double agent A spy working simultaneously for opposing intelligence services in two or more countries.
encryption The process by which text, voice, or data messages are scrambled to keep them secret.

Glossary

EYC The European Youth Coalition.

federalists Those who advocate a form of government in which a union of states recognizes a central authority while maintaining their powers to govern themselves.

front group A fake organization designed to gather intelligence or influence public opinion.

GRU Glavnoye Razvedyvatelnoye Upravlenie, or Soviet military intelligence.

heir apparent The next person in line to inherit the British throne.

intelligence agent A person who gathers secret military and political information for a country's government.

intelligence network A group of agents who gather military and political secrets and pass them on to a superior.

IRA The Irish Republican Army.

ISC The International Student Coalition.

ISI The Inner-Service Intelligence, Pakistan's secret intelligence agency.

junta A group of people who seize control of a government after a revolution.

KGB Komitet Gosudarstvennoy Bezopasnosti, the secret intelligence service of the former Soviet Union.

Kremlin The government of the former Soviet Union.

League of Nations A world organization founded after World War I to promote international cooperation and peace. It existed between 1920 and 1946.

mandate A commission from the League of Nations authorizing a member nation to administer a territory.

MI5 Military Intelligence, Section 5, responsible for espionage within the borders of the United Kingdom.

MI6   Military Intelligence, Section 6, responsible for conducting espionage beyond the borders of the United Kingdom.

mole   A spy or double agent.

NCFE   The U.S. National Committee for a Free Europe.

NSA   The National Security Agency.

NSA   The National Student Association, used as a front to fight communism during the Cold War.

overt   Open and observable; not hidden.

PCO   The Passport Control Office in Great Britain.

SIS   The Secret Intelligence Service in Great Britain.

UB   Urzad Bezpieczenstwa, the Polish Secret Service.

For More Information

Greenpeace
702 H Street NW, Suite 300
Washington, DC 20001
(800) 326-0959
Web site: http://www.greenpeace.org

International Spy Museum
800 F Street NW
Washington, DC 20002
(866) SPY MUSEUM
Web site: http://www.spymuseum.org

SIS (MI6)
Enquiries Desk
P.O. Box 3255
London, England SW1P 1AE

SS (MI5)
Enquiries Desk
P.O. Box 3255
London, England SW1P 1AE

Terrorist Group Profiles
Dudley Knox Library
Naval Post Graduate School
411 Dyer Road
Montery, CA 93943
Web site: http://web.nps.navy.mil/~library/tgp/tgp2.htm

Web Sites

Due to the changing nature of Internet links, the Rosen Publishing Group, Inc., has developed an online list of Web sites related to the subject of this book. This site is updated regularly. Please use this link to access the list:

http://www.rosenlinks.com/iwmfia/mi6/

For Further Reading

Bower, Tom. *The Red Web: MI6 and the KGB Mastercoup.* London: Mandarin, 1993.

Dorril, Stephen. *MI6: Fifty Years of Special Operations.* London: Fourth Estate, 2000.

Dorril, Stephen. *MI6: Inside the Covert World of Her Majesty's Secret Intelligence Service.* New York: Simon and Schuster, 2000.

Fraser-Smith, Charles. *Secret Warriors: Hidden Heroes of MI6, OSS, MI9, SOE, and SAS.* Cumbia, England: Paternoster Press, 1984.

Geraghty, Tony. *The Irish War: The Hidden Conflict Between the IRA and British Intelligence.* Edited by Johns Hopkins. Baltimore: Johns Hopkins University Press, 2000.

Manley, Claudia B. *Secret Agents: Life as a Professional Spy.* New York: The Rosen Publishing Group, Inc., 2001.

Platt, Richard. *Spies!* (Eyewitness Books). New York: Dorling Kindersley, 2000.

Smith, Lou. *The Secret of MI6.* New York: St. Martin's Press, 1978.

West, Nigel. *MI6: British Secret Intelligence Service Operations 1909–1945.* New York: Random House, 1983.

West, Nigel. *The Secret War of the Falklands: The SAS, MI6 and the War Whitehall Nearly Lost.* London: Little Brown, 1997.

Bibliography

Bower, Tom. *The Red Web: MI6 and the KGB Mastercoup.* London: Mandarin, 1993.

British Broadcasting Company. "Spy Plans 'Threat to Human Rights.'" December 3, 2000. Retrieved February 28, 2002 (http://news.bbc.co.uk/hi/english/uk/newsid_1052000/1052341.stm).

Ctvnews.com. "MI6." Retrieved March 1, 2002 (http://www.ctvnews.com/content/publish/popups/war_on_terror/brief/agencies/agencies_content/mi6.htm).

Dorril, Stephen. *MI6: Fifty Years of Special Operations.* London: Fourth Estate, 2000.

Dorril, Stephen. *MI6: Inside the Covert World of Her Majesty's Secret Intelligence Service.* New York: Simon and Schuster.

Five.org. "MI5: Security Service." Retrieved March 2, 2002 (http://www.five.org.uk/security/mi5org/mi5org.htm).

Fraser-Smith, Charles. *Secret Warriors: Hidden Heroes of MI6, OSS, MI9, SOE, and SAS.* Cumbia, England: Paternoster Press, 1984.

Geraghty, Tony. *The Irish War: The Hidden Conflict Between the IRA and British Intelligence.* Edited by Johns Hopkins. Baltimore: Johns Hopkins University Press, 2000.

The Guardian. "MI6 Internet Purge Doomed to Failure." May 14, 1999. Retrieved March 1, 2002 (http://www.guardian.co.uk/uk_news/story/0,3604,298662,00.html).

Bibliography

Harris, Paul. *Sunday Herald.* "This War, More Than Any Other, Must Be a Battle of Electronic Spies in the Shadows." 2002. Retrieved February 25, 2002 (http://www.sundayherald.com/18651).

Knightley, Phillip. *The Second Oldest Profession.* New York: Penguin Books, 1988.

West, Nigel. *MI6: British Secret Intelligence Service Operations 1909–1945.* New York: Random House, 1983.

Wise, David, and Thomas B. Ross. *The Establishment.* New York: Random House, 1967.

Index

A
Al Qaeda, 38, 39, 50–52
Anschluss, 19–20

B
Boer War, the, 14
British Broadcasting Corporation
    (BBC), the, 24, 34
British intelligence
    agencies of, 4, 14, 16, 21
    between the World Wars, 16–20
    and code-breaking, 21
    domestic, 35, 39–44
    in the early twentieth century,
        14–15
    foreign, 35–39
    and Palestine, 18–19
    public image of, 5
    and World War I, 15–16
    and World War II, 19–21
British League for European
    Freedom, 24

C
carrier pigeons, 11
Central Intelligence Agency (CIA),
    4, 22, 26–31, 33
code-breaking, 21
Cold War, the, 22, 24–33
Committee of Imperial Defence
    (CID), 14
communism, 4, 17, 22, 31
counterespionage, 13, 16
Cuban Missile Crisis, the, 30–31
Cumming, Mansfield ("C"), 9–10,
    13, 16

D
Dalton, Hugh Reginald, 18–19
Dearlove, Richard Billing, 34–35, 46
double agents, 7, 28

E
Echelon spy satellite, 52
Enigma cryptographic machine, 21
European Movement (EM), the, 24, 25
European Youth Coalition (EYC), 26

F
Federal Bureau of Investigation
    (FBI), 41

G
Germany, 4, 10, 11, 12, 14, 15,
    17–22, 36
    annexation of Austria by,
        19–20
    division of Berlin, 22
    Nazis in, 17–18, 19–21
    persecution of Jews by, 18–19
Gestapo, the, 19, 20

H
Hall, Reginald ("Blinker"), 14, 15
Hezbollah, 38–39
Hitler, Adolf, 17–18

I
Imperial Security Intelligence
    Service (MO5), 16
intelligence
    early methods of, 11
    establishing agencies, 4, 6–7
    and technology, 6, 52

Index

Internet, the, 45–47, 53
Ireland, 8, 42

K
Kendrick, Thomas, 19–20
KGB, 28, 29, 31

L
League of Nations, 18

M
MI1, 16
MI5, 16, 35, 36, 39–44
    duties of, 41–42
    methods of, 43–44
MI6
    and the CIA, 26–31, 33
    and the Cold War, 24–33
    changes to, 32–33
    duties of, 35–36
    future of, 45–53
    and the Internet, 45–47
    leadership of, 34–35, 46
    methods of, 36–39
    origins of, 4, 5, 9–13, 16
    and the Soviet Union, 22, 24, 26, 28, 36
    and terrorism, 38–39, 48–53
    units of, 16
    and the U.S., 26–31
    and World War II, 19–21
MI8, 21
Military Intelligence's Signals Intelligence (MISI), 21
MO5, 16

N
National Committee for a Free Europe (NCFE), 24
Naval Intelligence Division (NID), 4, 11
Nazis, 17–18, 19–21
Northern Ireland, 42

P
Palestine, 17–19
Penkovsky, Oleg, 28–31
propaganda, 16, 31

R
Royal Navy, 4, 9, 14, 16
Russia, 4, 15, 16, 17, 22, 28, 30, 36, 38

S
Secret Intelligence Service (SIS), 4, 5, 18, 19, 21
    foreign offices of, 13
    early history of, 9–13, 16
Secret Service Committee, the, 16
Sinclair, Hugh, 16–17
Soviet Union (USSR), the, 22, 24, 26, 33, 36
    and Cuba, 30–31
    and intelligence, 28, 29
    and the U.S., 30–31
surveillance, 42, 52

T
telephone tapping, 43

U
United Kingdom
    formation of, 8
    Labour Party in, 9
    monarchy in, 8–9
    and Palestine, 17–19
    Parliament of, 9
    prime minister of, 9, 21, 32

W
World War I, 10–12, 15–16
World War II, 4, 19–21, 22, 33

Credits

About the Author

Shaun McCormack lives in New Jersey, where he graduated from Montclair State University. A journalist, he has written several books for the Rosen Publishing Group.

Photo Credits

Cover © AP/Wide World Photos; pp. 5, 7, 12, 15, 17, 19, 23, 25, 28, 30, 32, 44 © Hulton/Archive/Getty Images, Inc.; pp. 8, 39, 49 © Reuters New Media, Inc./Corbis; p. 20 © Corbis; pp. 26, 29 © Bettmann/Corbis; p. 37 © Peter Turnley/Corbis; p. 40 © Francoise De Mulder/Corbis; p. 46 © Reuters/Dan Cheung/Corbis; p. 51 © AFP/Corbis.

Layout and Design

Thomas Forget

Editor

Jill Jarnow

www.ingramcontent.com/pod-product-compliance
Lightning Source LLC
Chambersburg PA
CBHW041115070526
44584CB00002B/178